Sea Monsters

by Christine Kohler

The ocean is filled with countless beautiful wonders, but did you know that strange creatures also live in its darkness? Some are highly poisonous, and a few behave oddly. Others look like they belong in a horror movie!

The Box Jellyfish

One of the deadliest sea monsters is the box jellyfish. It lives in parts of the Indian and Pacific oceans. It has long, thin parts around its mouth. These parts carry a powerful sting that helps to protect the jellyfish from enemies, or **predators**. Because these jellyfish are nearly see-through, divers must remain alert to avoid them.

Box jellyfish have long, deadly string-like parts near the mouth.

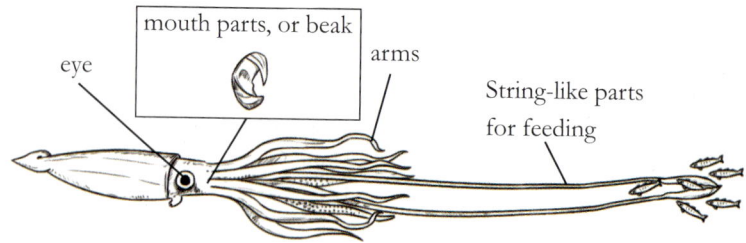

A colossal squid

The Colossal Squid

The word *colossal* means "huge." However, the colossal squid is not the biggest animal in the ocean. That title goes to the blue whale, the largest animal to have ever lived on Earth. But the squid is still big—each of its eyes is the size of a soccer ball. It also has eight arms and string-like parts it uses to catch fish and drag them to its mouth.

The colossal squid lives more than a mile beneath icy waters near Antarctica. It is seldom seen. In fact, for centuries, people thought the animal might be a **legend**, or story. Then one was caught in 2007. The captured squid was thirty feet long!

A colossal squid uses its arms to grab its prey.

Goblin Sharks

One of the oldest fish in the ocean is the goblin shark. It has been around for over 100 million years.

It's easy to see how the goblin got its name. It hunts in the deep sea for food, or **prey**. To grab its prey, the shark's jaw and fifty sharp teeth shoot forward from its mouth! It looks like something from a nightmare.

The goblin shark

Female anglerfish trick prey with the worm-like growth on their heads.

The Anglerfish

The anglerfish could win the prize for the ugliest sea creature. It's flabby and lumpy and lives deep in the ocean. The females have a strange growth on top of their heads that looks like a worm. It helps them attract, or **lure**, prey to their giant mouths.

Whenever you look at an ocean, remember. Monsters aren't just in movies. They also live deep in the sea!